Associative Reasoning A

Dr. DooRiddles
A3

SERIES TITLES
Dr. DooRiddles
A1 ▪ A2 ▪ A3
B1 ▪ B2
C1
Spelling DooRiddles
A1 • B1

Written by
John H. Doolittle

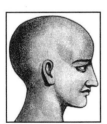

© 2005
THE CRITICAL THINKING CO.™
www.CriticalThinking.com
Phone: 800-458-4849 • Fax: 831-393-3277
P.O. Box 1610 • Seaside • CA 93955-1610
ISBN 978-0-89455-878-8

SUSTAINABLE FORESTRY INITIATIVE
Certified Fiber Sourcing
www.sfiprogram.org

ABOUT THE AUTHOR

John Doolittle has been a professor of psychology at California State University, Sacramento since 1966. He received a bachelor's degree in biology and psychology from Stanford University, a master's degree in psychology from San Jose State University, and a doctoral degree in experimental psychology from the University of Colorado, Boulder. At Sacramento, Dr. Doolittle has taught in the schools of Education, Arts and Sciences, and Engineering and Computer Science. He has also been a visiting professor at the University of Melbourne, Australia. Dr. Doolittle is author of a number of books and software published by The Critical Thinking Co.™, including *Revenge of the Riddle Spiders* software, the *Dr. DooRiddle Associative Reasoning* series, and *Spelling DooRiddles*.

TEACHING SUGGESTIONS

Everyone loves the mystery of a riddle and *Dr. DooRiddles* will bring laughter, groans, and challenges (perhaps for as much as a week or more per riddle) to you and your students.

Thinking Skills

Perceiving relationships between words, ideas, and concepts is called associative reasoning, which is a skill necessary for creative thought. Riddle solving requires students to use important skills of associative, inductive, and divergent thinking to find the answers. Students will learn to recognize important ideas, examine these ideas from different points of view, and then find connections between the ideas. These teachable skills are essential for efficient, successful, open-ended problem solving of all kinds.

Role of the Student

Although *Dr. DooRiddles* are fun and tantalizing, answering them is not simple play. In order to solve these riddles, students have to generate solutions in many different categories. Students often confuse multiple-category generation of answers with offering the same answer rephrased. To clarify this confusion, students need to learn how to examine an idea from many reference points.

For Example:

> If one of the given clues in a riddle were the word *horn*, students would have to think of different meanings and applications of that word. Does it refer to a kind of musical instrument? a part of an animal? to the geographic term? a general horn shape? or does it refer to an alternative in a dilemma?

Role of the Teacher

At first, the teacher will need to help the students learn how to produce multiple-category solutions by asking higher level thinking questions. Eventually, responsibility of self-questioning should be turned over to the students. Teach your students to ask themselves questions such as: How is the clue used? Why is it phrased this way? Is this clue connected to a clue in another line? How else can this word be spelled? Is this a whole word or a partial words? Does this line mean what it says or is it a play on words? Does this word sound like another word?

Students should be encouraged to "listen" to the riddles, examining the sound of each line and individual words, and to use visual imagery to "see" what's happening. As they get into the process of riddle solving, they will learn to read and weigh the importance of each word in each line so they can interpret the clues correctly. They will learn to notice how highly descriptive adjectives, verbs, and adverbs indicate specific kinds of movement or action; and how unusual phonetic spellings, homonyms, prefixes, suffixes, roots, puns, analogies, and multiple word meanings are used to both hide and reveal the clues.

Always ask students why they chose the answer they did. Do not allow students to just give their answer without explaining the reasoning behind it. When answers are backed up and evaluated in group discussions, class members share their knowledge, connect it to other ideas and explore the concept in many directions to find a "best" answer from among possible multiple answers. By working and sharing information in groups, children who are not familiar with the culture, or who lack English proficiency, will expand their knowledge, build more extensive vocabulary, and will be able to apply information more diversely.

Classroom Application

These materials make great sponge activities and are excellent activities for independent, cooperative, or open learning situations. The riddles can be used as part of the daily thinking skill curriculum or for the challenge of the week. The riddles spiral up in difficulty within each book and from level to level so that teachers may select the appropriate level of difficulty for students.

Dr. DooRiddles cuts across curriculum areas and deals with real-world objects and situations. Both teachers and students will find the mind-broadening strategies used in these challenging activities richly rewarding at test-taking time.

ANSWERS

Page 1
egg
brick (s)
boy

Page 2
brother
brown
bulb

Page 3
clouds
door
draw

Page 4
Earth
eat
even

Page 5
facts
family
field

Page 6
fire
first
friend

Page 7
front
games
green

Page 8
ground
grows
half

Page 9
letters
little
money

Page 10
moon
night
old

Page 11
round
talk, converse
water

Page 12
winter
A
flowers

Page 13
hospital
hot
huge

Page 14
hurry
idea
job

Page 15
kitchen
laugh
lid

Page 16
lines
listen
locked

Page 17
broom
pot
trunk

Page 18
suitcase
match
mouse

Page 19
bat
stairs
chain

Page 20
spider
nails
web

Page 21
candlestick (candle)
pole
clown

Page 22
ticket
peanuts
hot dog (s)

Page 23
gum
rope
pail

Page 24
brush
hay
coffee

Page 25
sugar
bacon
shovel

Page 26
clock
hat
pen

Page 27
desk / pencil box
calendar
sail

Page 28
king
throne
recipe

Page 29
robe
deer
crow

Page 30
sheep / lamb
arrow
hammer

Page 31
seagulls
map
shell

Page 32
towel
umbrella
cannon

Page 33
gold
moon
rake

Page 34
lies
mix
autumn

Page 35
carrot
ate / eight
add

Page 36
afraid / scared
after
all

Page 37
animals
band
bang (s)

Page 38
fortune
library
snack

Page 39
tent
gas
axe

Page 40
bees
best
bite (s)

Page 41
beast
beets, beats
castle (s)

Page 42
farm

MODEL LESSON

My tail can wag,
My feet there are four;
I scratch or bark,
When I want out the door.

Each line, or pair of lines, in the above riddle contains a clue to the answer. Carefully read each line and try to figure out what is being described. Look for clue words. Try to form a picture in your mind as you connect all the clues. Ask yourself questions about each of the clues.

For Example:

In the first line, *tail* and *wag* are clue words. What has a tail and wags it?

In the second line, *four feet* are clue words. What has four feet and a tail that can wag?

In the third line, *scratch* and *bark* are clue words. What scratches and barks?

In the fourth line, *want out the door* goes with scratch and bark. What scratches and barks when it wants out the door?

Now how would you connect all the clues? Perhaps the first thing that comes to mind as an answer is a dog. Let's see if dog works. A dog does have a tail, and it wags it when it is happy. A dog does have four feet. When a dog wants to go out, it often scratches or barks to let its owner know. So dog does fit all the clues and it is a good answer. Someone else may come up with a different answer, and if it fits all the clues, it is also a good answer.

I have a white shell,
That's easy to crack;
I'm good for breakfast,
Or even a snack.

What am I? ....

For fireplace or patio,
My red blocks will look nice;
The pig who built his house of me,
Sure made that wolf think twice.

What am I? ....

Another word for lad,
I'm younger than a man;
With cow I ride a horse,
With scout I lend a hand.

What am I? ....

In families I'm found,
The opposite of sister;
You should be thinking male,
You should be thinking mister.

What am I? ....

The color of dirt,
I'm five letters long;
Think about chocolate,
And you can't go wrong.

What am I? ....

Plant me in the ground,
And see a flower grow;
Or else, flip the switch,
And I will start to glow.

What am I? ....

Although I'm not smoke,
I'm puffs in the sky;
And if I am dark,
You may not stay dry.

What am I? ....

Stay out if I am shut,
Come in if I am open;
If you forget the key,
Then, someone's home, you're hopin'.

What am I? ....

If you would make a picture,
I am what must be done;
Take paper and a pencil,
And then just have some fun.

What am I? ....

Set in the universe,
I am our planet home;
A rocket you will need,
If you would like to roam.

What am I? ....

Put food into your mouth,
Don't forget to swallow;
And when your plate is empty,
Dessert will surely follow.

What am I? ....

The opposite of odd,
With me the sides are fair;
When the things are me,
They're easier to share.

What am I? ....

You look for me in books,
The ones that are not fiction;
When you know all of me,
You can speak with conviction.

What am I? ....

You're born into my tree,
It bears your father's name;
Think relatives of yours,
Whose last names are the same.

What am I? ....

My out in baseball lies,
Quite far from the home plate;
A place for cows to graze,
And chew and ruminate.

What am I? ....

My truck can be yellow,
But mostly it is red;
When I am in my place,
With logs I can be fed.

What am I? ....

The opposite of last,
My place is in the lead;
And if you stay in me,
You surely will succeed.

What am I? ....

Another word for pal,
Or buddy or for mate;
When put with boy or girl,
You could be on a date.

What am I? ....

The opposite of back,
My weather's moving in;
And so it's with my page,
Newspapers must begin.

What am I? ....

Think video or football,
Think checkers or Old Maid,
Think soccer or think hopscotch;
For all these things are played.

What am I? ....

The color of U.S. money,
The color of some trees;
The color of spring leaves,
Seen moving with the breeze.

What am I? ....

With beef I make a burger,
My floor is at the bottom;
Where falling leaves are headed,
When summer turns to autumn.

What am I? ....

I'm what an acorn does,
A mighty oak to be;
The opposite of shrinks,
The answer, do you see?

What am I? ....

If the split is equal,
Then both kids will get me;
I'm more than a quarter,
But less than whole, you see?

What am I? ....

The twenty-six of us,
Whom every kid must know;
Or, you will need some stamps,
Without them, we won't go.

What am I? ....

The opposite of big,
The opposite of tall;
Now, please do not think short,
And please do not think small.

What am I? ....

I'm the coin of the realm,
The dollar and the cent;
When you went to the mall,
I was the stuff you spent.

What am I? ....

I can be full,
Or I can be new;
In the night sky,
I shine down on you.

What am I? ....

Darkness all around,
The sun has long since gone;
You should be asleep,
Aha! I saw you yawn.

What am I? ....

The opposite of young,
The opposite of new;
And please do not think used,
Whatever else you do.

What am I? ....

The shape of most doughnuts,
And pies that you see;
The shape of a circle,
Or merry-go-me.

What am I? ....

If you start to speak,
Then I am what you do;
Someone hears your words,
And says some back to you.

What am I? ....

When you wash your face,
I fill up the sink;
Or, when you are dry,
I am what you drink.

What am I? ....

Not summer, not fall,
The season of snow;
Dress warmly, old friend,
When chilly winds blow.

What am I? ....

A very good grade,
There isn't one better;
In the alphabet,
I am the first letter.

What am I? ....

We're roses, we're daisies,
We're tulips, we're mums;
And lots of us bloom,
As soon as spring comes.

What am I? ....

I'm where the kid is born,
If Dad can start the car;
With doctors and nurses,
And patients under par.

What am I? ....

I am the temperature,
Of burners when they're on;
And if the sun is me,
Try shade until it's gone.

What am I? ....

I start with an 'H',
Four letters are in me;
Think bigger than big,
And then you soon will see.

What am I? ....

I'm what you're in,
When you rush about;
"Hey, where's the fire?"
You hear someone shout.

What am I? ....

Another word for notion,
I pop into your head;
I'm kind of like a short dream,
But you are not in bed.

What am I? ....

Another word for task,
Another word for chore;
Think doctor, think lawyer,
Teacher or janitor.

What am I? ....

I'm where you can go,
To see food prepared;
Where carrots are peeled,
And apples are pared.

What am I? ....

When someone tells a joke,
A happy sound you make;
If I am done too much,
Your sides will start to ache.

What am I? ....

Put me back on the jar,
The mayonnaise won't spoil;
Put me on a saucepan;
When stuff starts to boil.

What am I? ....

I am what you must learn,
For your part in the play;
When coloring that book,
Inside me try to stay.

What am I? ....

I am what you must do,
So teacher can be heard;
Do me with all your might,
And you won't miss a word.

What am I? ....

Sorry, you can't enter,
Each time the door is me;
You just have to hope,
That someone has a key.

What am I? ....

You use me to sweep,
The dirt from the floor;
My handle is long,
To help with the chore.

What am I? ....

When filled with good things,
I'm used to make stew;
Or fill me with dirt,
And blooms, red and blue.

What am I? ....

A large box you fill,
When you go to sea;
An elephant has one,
And so does a tree.

What am I? ....

You put your clothes in me,
When you go on a trip;
With wheels you can roll,
And handle you can grip.

What am I? ....

I rhyme well with catch,
Your fire to start;
Those who play with me,
Are not very smart.

What am I? ....

I really like cheese,
I make folks say "Eek!"
But when I see cats,
I run with a "Squeak."

What am I? ....

The one that flies blind,
But doesn't get hurt;
Or goes with a ball,
Some players and dirt.

What am I? ....

From one floor to another,
I'm steps you must be taking;
But if my flights are too long,
Your legs will soon be aching.

What am I? ....

I have a lot of links,
I'm mostly made of steel;
And I will lock your bike,
When wrapped 'round a wheel.

What am I? ....

I have eight long legs,
And use them to crawl;
Look up in the air,
See me on the wall.

What am I? ....

Builders will work,
To hammer me down;
I hold together,
The walls of this town.

What am I? ....

A spider's home,
I'm woven with care;
My silken threads,
Are as light as air.

What am I? ....

Jack was quick,
Jumping over me;
I'm a stick,
Made of wax, you see.

What am I? ....

In the North I stand,
Next to Santa's dwelling;
I'm seen with a flag,
And 'P' starts my spelling.

What am I? ....

My shoes are big and floppy,
A red ball is my nose;
I'll bet I can make you laugh,
Dressed in my funny clothes.

What am I? ....

A little piece of paper,
That may say, "Admit one;"
You give me to the taker,
Then, go enjoy the fun.

What am I? ....

All elephants remember,
I'm what they love to eat;
My butter mixed with jelly,
Will make a tasty treat.

What am I? ....

You love me at the ballpark,
Or at the barbecue;
With mustard in a long bun,
I sure taste good to you.

What am I? ....

Don't chew me in church,
Don't chew me at school;
Me stuck to your shoe,
Is really not cool.

What am I? ....

They tie me in knots,
I'm bigger than string;
When tied to that tree,
I help make a swing.

What am I? ....

I'm a kind of bucket,
As used by Jack and Jill;
My guess is I was dropped,
When they fell down the hill.

What am I? ....

I start with 'B',
I'm held in your hand;
Use me to scrub,
As hard as you can.

What am I? ....

I'm found in a barn,
A horse's lunch today;
Needles in my stack,
Are not found right away.

What am I? ....

Some grown-ups like me,
To help them wake up;
And some prefer tea,
To have in their cup.

What am I? ....

I grew up in a cane,
I can be brown or white;
I make that food taste sweet,
I know you'd like a bite.

What am I? ....

I sizzle in the pan,
The 'B' in BLT;
For breakfast I am served,
With eggs and toast, you see.

What am I? ....

A tool that is used,
For digging around;
To break through the earth,
And scoop up the ground.

What am I? ....

My hands don't grab,
My face won't sour;
You'll look for me,
To find the hour.

What am I? ....

I sit on your head,
And keep out the sun;
I go with cowboy,
And holster and gun.

What am I? ....

I can be ballpoint,
Or felt tip or quill;
And you can use me,
To write what you will.

What am I? ....

A workplace for you,
In your classroom lies;
Now, lift up the top,
And see your supplies.

What am I? ....

You can look straight at me,
And, then, find out the date;
And count how many days,
For summer, you must wait.

What am I? ....

When I'm blown full,
The wind moves the boat;
When I'm pulled down,
The boat will just float.

What am I? ....

The leader of the land,
The husband of the queen;
And in time of battle,
I try hard to look mean.

What am I? ....

I'm where the king sits,
To rule o'er the land;
You see, if you're king,
You don't have to stand.

What am I? ....

The notes you follow,
When learning to cook;
Be sure to find me,
I'm found in a book.

What am I? ....

Mom wears hers over nightclothes,
The judge wears his in court;
And Dad could never wear yours,
It would be way too short.

What am I? ....

The larger one's a buck,
The smaller one's a doe;
Little fawns will follow,
Wherever she may go.

What am I? ....

With "scare" I'm a man,
Who is stuffed with straw;
Alone I'm a bird,
That laughs with a "caw."

What am I? ....

My fur is called wool,
And it grows very thick;
I show that I'm mad,
With a "baa" and a kick.

What am I? ....

I am a wooden stick,
With feathers on the end;
But before I am shot,
A bow will have to bend.

What am I? ....

I'm used to pound nails,
Or else pull them out;
But when I hit a thumb,
You'll really hear a shout.

What am I? ....

We're large shore birds,
Who must like to screech;
Dogs will often chase us,
When they're on the beach.

What am I? ....

A large piece of paper,
To guide you on your way;
I'm really hard to fold,
For use another day.

What am I? ....

I once was the home,
Of oyster or clam;
Find me by the sea,
And guess what I am.

What am I? ....

I am a large cloth,
You can use for drying;
But here on the beach,
On me you'll be lying.

What am I? ....

I'm not just for rain,
I keep out the sun;
You sit under me,
When having beach fun.

What am I? ....

A powerful gun on,
The deck of a ship;
And I'm much too large,
To wear on your hip.

What am I? ....

You'll find me in rings,
Worn by Mom and Dad;
And nuggets of me,
Make miners feel glad.

What am I? ....

Up in the sky,
I rise in the night;
When I am full,
I give lots of light.

What am I? ....

A tool you can use,
For leaves on the ground;
Unlike a blower,
I don't make a sound.

What am I? ....

The opposite of truth,
We shouldn't have been said;
Or, think of a baby,
Just sleeping on his bed.

What am I? ....

A box with the stuff,
You need for a cake;
Add water and eggs,
You're ready to bake.

What am I? ....

The season of the year,
When trees will drop their leaves;
Another word for fall,
Wear sweaters with long sleeves.

What am I? ....

A vegetable orange,
Much loved by the rabbit;
Eat me for a snack,
A very good habit.

What am I? ....

What you did to your meal,
Just last night at dinner;
Guess a number less than nine,
And you may be a winner.

What am I? ....

You do me to numbers,
My sign is a plus;
I'll give you a sum,
With very little fuss.

What am I? ....

I am what you feel,
When something is scary;
A feeling of fear,
Of things big and hairy.

What am I? ....

Happily forever,
They both lived me;
Think: "What's not before?"
Then, you will see.

What am I? ....

Along with "or nothing,"
There is no in between;
Combine me with "alone,"
No one else will be seen.

What am I? ....

You see us on the farm,
You see us at the zoo;
And, yes, at the circus,
And in the forest, too.

What am I? ....

With rock we make music,
Your hearing we harm;
And, with watch I help time,
To stay on your arm.

What am I? ....

Mom cuts her nice hair,
Just above her eyes;
The sounds the gun made,
Were quite a surprise.

What am I? ....

Another word for luck,
At carnivals I'm told;
A treasure chest of jewels,
With silver and with gold.

What am I? ....

You go to me for books,
And never have to pay;
Unless you don't return,
The book on its due day.

What am I? ....

A small amount of food,
So you can last 'til lunch;
I'm not a full meal,
But just a little munch.

What am I? ....

Take me on camping trips,
And I'm a portable home;
I'm used by the circus,
So the animals won't roam.

What am I? ....

I am fuel for your car,
And with me you can drive;
Buy me at the station,
To keep the car alive.

What am I? ....

If a tree needs chopping,
I'm the tool that you need;
Beware of my sharp edge,
This warning you should heed.

What am I? ....

We're busy insects,
Our homes are called hives;
If we are killers,
All run for your lives!

What am I? ....

Better than good,
And better than better;
When you are this,
You're quite a go-getter.

What am I? ....

If you don't take care,
I'm what mosquitoes do;
You do me to an apple,
Before you, then, can chew.

What am I? ....

You've heard me paired with Beauty,
In that loved fairy tale;
Or I prowl the jungle,
With tooth and claw and tail.

What am I? ....

Red slices of me,
Make salads a treat;
With drum we are not,
Something you can eat.

What am I? ....

The home of kings and queens,
With drawbridges and moats;
Where knights can ride around,
Dressed up in their steel coats.

What am I? ....

Cows, pigs, and chickens,
Can make their home on me;
Tractors, barns, and fields;
Are also there to see.

What am I? ....